MARKETIN AUTOMATION

Automate Your Business through Marketing Best Practices such as Email Marketing and Search Engine optimization

BOOK DESCRIPTION

Marketing automation has revolutionalized the way business firms carry out their marketing efforts. This has resulted in lower marketing costs, lean and efficient marketing team, higher return-on-investment (ROI) on marketing effort and higher revenue streams. Yet, these and many other benefits seem to be a preserve of the few well-informed large enterprises. Many small and medium-sized enterprises shy away from marketing automation either due to lack of awareness or failure to understand how it can transform their marketing operations.

This book specifically endeavors to demystify marketing automation, create awareness of what marketing automation is, and encourage small-scale and medium-sized enterprises to employ this great technology for their very own survival and competitive advantage. We have provided a host of free marketing automation tools so that there is no excuse whatsoever not to grow and earn more.

You will not only get to know about the unique benefits of marketing automation that you have been missing, but also get to know which tools are best suited for your type of business, when and how to implement them.

There is much more than you ought to know. Kindly download or request a print copy of this book to switch your business to a higher growth gear.

Enjoy reading!

ABOUT THE AUTHOR

George Pain is an entrepreneur, author and business consultant. He specializes in setting up online businesses from scratch, investment income strategies and global mobility solutions. He has successfully built several businesses from the ground up and is excited to share his knowledge with you.

DISCLAIMER

CONTENTS

INTRODUCTION

Many businesses waste their resources on inefficient and ineffective marketing efforts leading to frustration and loss of marketing opportunities. A good number of them are not aware that technologies exist to help them reduce waste, streamline their resources and engage in highly efficient and effective marketing effort to boost their marketing return-on-investment (ROI) effort. Marketing automation is the solution.

This book provides in-depth information on marketing automation. It shows how a business firm (whether small, medium-sized, or large) can apply marketing automation and thus be able to cut on cost, boost productivity, increase marketing ROI and gain higher revenues.

Keep reading!

WHAT IS MARKETING AUTOMATION?

Marketing is the most important function of any business enterprise. Without a market, a business cannot exist. Yet, there are plenty of lost opportunities due to inefficiency and ineffectiveness of marketing effort.

The following are the ways by which marketing opportunities get lost or frustrated:

- Inability to scale up to meet increasing demand
- Inability to find new leads (potential customers) due to limited marketing scope
- Inability to convert potential leads into buying customers
- Inability to get customer feedback to improve on the marketing effort
- Poor and untimely response to customers' needs due to a limited scope
- Inability to carry out in-depth market analysis to gain a deeper insight of what the market wants
- Expensive cost of marketing labor
- Inability to diversify marketing channels
- Inability to carry out repetitive marketing tasks in an efficient and effective manner

Lost marketing opportunities simply mean lost revenue. Marketing automation is a technology that has come about to ensure that marketing effort is not lost or frustrated due to operational limitations.

Definition of marketing automation

Marketing automation refers to technological use software to manage, execute and automate marketing tasks and processes.

The rationale for marketing automation

With marketing automation, you can streamline your online marketing effort, automate routine processes, acquire real-time analytics, optimize your outreach engagement, and gather actionable intelligence. This enables you to scale up your sales and marketing efforts more effectively and efficiently.

Streamlined marketing effort include market segmentation, up-selling and cross-selling, customer lifecycle marketing, customer retention, lead management, and marketing ROI measurement. Lead management includes lead generation, lead scoring, and lead nurturing.

Marketing automation platforms

Marketing automation is about letting technology take over functions that are handled more effectively and efficiently by software rather than human beings. Since marketing automation software requires sophisticated skills and resources to build, run and maintain; it is hardly feasible for businesses (especially small-scale businesses) to have their own in-house marketing software. Thus, various independent marketing platforms offer a range of software, tools, resources and requisite skilled workforce to maintain them. These specialized technology enterprises offer marketing automation Platform-as-a-Service (PAAS) to other businesses.

Common Features of Marketing Automation Platforms

There are dozens of marketing automation platforms today. Each platform has its own differentiating features. However, there are those common basic features that must exist for them to be termed as marketing automation platforms.

The following are typical features of a marketing automation platform:

- Content management – Allows creation, curation, customization, and delivery of content through various channels tailored to the need of a specific audience.

- Email Marketing – Allows automated scheduling and release of email to the target audience
- Campaign Management – Provides automated sending of emails based on user behavior
- Forms – Offers built-in registration forms connected directly to your own database
- Landing Pages – Creates customized landing pages per specific campaign
- CRM Integration – Facilitates automated data syncing and custom profile creation
- Social Media management – Allows posting, sharing, listening and tracking on multiple social accounts
- Lead Management– Manages leads based on behavior
- SEO & Keyword research – Allows keyword research, keyword campaigns, and optimization of your content for the search engine. This is an optional feature to consider, as it is not key to all platforms, yet very important.
- Analytics – Reports dashboard with various analytics reporting parameters e.g. revenue, visits, reactions, etc

Marketing automation prerequisites

For marketing automation to succeed, the following must be part of its critical ingredients:

- **Central Marketing Database** – A marketing database is a system of record that has an accumulated collection of essential marketing data such as customers' details and interactions, and prospects' details and their behaviors. This can enable you to develop segmentation criteria to provide a customized solution for each segment.
- **Engagement Marketing Engine** – This is the central processing unit (CPU) of marketing automation. It is where creation, automation, and management of marketing processes and conversations across various channels take place.
- **Analytics Engine** – This is where standardization (establishing parameters), measurement, control, and feedback take place. We can call it the control unit (CU) of marketing automation.

Basic Marketing Automation Strategy

A strategy is important in every business endeavor. Marketing being the most critical element of business, it needs no emphasis to prove the importance of strategy in marketing. Furthermore, when it comes to marketing automation, strategy becomes its lifeline.

The following are simple steps that help build a basic marketing automation strategy and advance it further as you gain more insight and experience:

- Step 1: Set and prioritize your goals
- Step 2: Map out your customer journey
- Step 3: Identify, demarcate and define your customer segments
- Step 4: Critically assess your content
- Step 5: Customize your message content creation and delivery to specific segments

Set and prioritize your goals

The following are goals that you may aim to achieve in your marketing automation endeavor:

- Increased brand awareness
- Increased customer engagement
- Increased customer loyalty
- Increased lead generation

Prioritize your goals to rank them in the order of importance to your marketing endeavor. This can help find the most appropriate marketing automation platform for your needs. Choose a marketing automation strategy that optimizes the achievement of set goals.

Map out your customer journey

The customer journey is market by three critical stages:

- Awareness
- Consideration
- Decision

Observe customer behavior as they walk along the journey through these critical stages. Keep note of their experiences and emotions at each stage. Seek to identify how your product can be a solution to their pains at each stage of their journey.

Identify, demarcate and define your customer segments

When it comes to marketing, a universal solution is no solution at all. Different kinds of customers require specific solutions. Thus, to reach to that level where you can provide a customized solution to their uniquely specific pain points, you have to identify each customer type, demarcate them into segments and clearly define each of these segments in terms of problems (pain points) and matching solutions.

Critically assess your content

There is no content that can be deemed fit for all. We all have different tastes and preferences. We are attracted to different flavors. There are those that desire content that is factual to the point. On the other hand, there are those who desire content that triggers emotions. Yet, there are those in-between.

Tune your content to suit specific customer segments that you have identified. Use marketing automation tools to identify customer behavior in order to recognize which segment they belong to and unleash appropriate content delivery.

More importantly, critically assess your content in terms of validity, reliability, and effectiveness in terms of meeting customer's informational needs, satisfying pain points and achieving your overall marketing goals.

Customize your message content creation and delivery to specific segments

The best way to customize your message content creation and delivery to target segments is to create message map.

The message map should have a flowchart that clearly shows the kind of message packets to deliver to each market segment. Each message packet should be clearly defined in terms of intent, message features, target segment, and goals. Then, each packet should link to a respective content delivery schedule. This is a great way to plan your messages.

Getting started with marketing automation

Knowing marketing automation is one thing, making the daring step to get started is another thing altogether. How does one get started?

Getting started is not hard at all. What you need is to make baby-steps and you are already into it. The following are the baby-steps to enable you to get started:

1. Identify your needs
2. Research on the most suitable marketing automation platform
3. Test it using a free-trial version
4. Get in touch with the relevant team in charge of your chosen platform
5. Procure the platform
6. Automate your marketing tasks

Identify your needs

What are those marketing tasks that you are currently performing that you think will be better off being automated? The following are common tasks that can be automated:

- Social media posting, engagement, and analytics
- Email marketing
- Landing pages creation
- Content generation and curation
- Web page creation
- Keyword research
- Search engine optimization (SEO)

Research on the most suitable marketing automation platform

There exist dozens of marketing automation platforms out there plus hundreds of independent automation tools for specific tasks. We have provided information on these tools in our last section.

Test using a free-trial version

Most of the marketing automation platforms have a free trial version. Use the free-trial version to test how the marketing automation platform works. Testing will help you know what works and what does not work in terms of your marketing function. Testing also enables you to know what kind of customization you will need to ask in order to suit your particular marketing needs.

Get in touch with the relevant team in charge of your chosen platform

Once you have tried several platforms and got the one that best fit your marketing automation needs, the next logical thing to do is to the get in touch with a representative of the respective platform. Explain to the representative your goals, the outcome of your test, and your own experience in carrying it out. Also, explain whether your goals are met or not and what you would like to be considered if there is a desire by them to satisfy your goals. Seek to know if there are other features that exist to enable you to achieve your goals in a much more efficient and effective way.

It is not common to find a marketing automation platform that will suit all your needs. Thus, you have to consider key priorities and tradeoff with regard to your goals and budget.

Procure the platform

Once you are satisfied with what the platform is offering, you can now go ahead and procure the platform. Most of the platforms only need you to register, subscribe and log in. Everything else is done on the hosted platform. However, there are a few of them (mostly specific tools as opposed to a platform) which you can download and host on your own.

Automate your marketing tasks

Once you have procured the platform, you can now configure it to your needs and automate your various marketing tasks. Each platform has its own User Instruction Manual. The technical representatives will also be available to help whenever there is a need.

DIFFERENT TYPES OF MARKETING AUTOMATION

The importance of marketing automation to online businesses has increased demand for marketing automation tools. However, before acquiring a marketing automation tool, it is important to acquaint yourself with the different types of marketing automation to be able to determine which area of your marketing process that needs automation and the type of automation that is best suited for it.

There are three main types of marketing automation:

1. Marketing intelligence
2. Business development
3. Workflow automation

Marketing intelligence

Marketing intelligence is the process of gathering disparate marketing data, synthesizing it, collating it and analyzing it against a set of specific KPIs to gain critical insight that can enable informed decision-making.

With zillions of bytes of data available online, the internet has become a huge data farm. Thus, it becomes more sensible for business firms to automate marketing intelligence to acquire this data not only internally but also externally.

Internally, the business can acquire this data from landing forms, websites, and points of sale. Externally, a business can acquire this data from email and social media interactions.

Marketing automation software uses tracking codes to monitor online behaviors of both customers and prospects. These behaviors can then be analyzed to identify behavioral patterns that can be segmented. This will result in behavior-based market segments.

Business development

Business development refers to ideas, activities, and initiatives geared towards optimizing business performance to achieve greater results.

The core activities of business development are:

- Business growth and expansion
- Building strategic partnerships
- Making strategic decisions
- Increasing revenues

Thus, business development is about identifying business opportunities, creating new partnerships and enhancing existing ones, finding alternative marketing channels, and products re-engineering to serve the existing markets in a better way.

Business development cuts across and collaborates with different layers of the organization structure that deals with the entire production process including product creation ideas, product marketing, product management, vendor management and product sales.

When it comes to marketing automation, business development focuses on the entire sales funnel right from the top (product awareness) to the bottom (closing the sale). It involves CRM - market segmentation, and lead management (generation, scoring, nurturing, and conversion). Automated business development will employ email management, social media management, search marketing (SEM & SEO), and content marketing to find ideas, optimize business performance and generate great results.

Other activities involved in automated business development include:

- Market research
- Salesforce automation
- CRM

- Pricing automation
- Branding management
- Distribution management
- Omni-channel management
- Operations management

Workflow automation

The term 'workflow' refers to a sequential flow of work based on structured methods, patterns and activities with the aim of achieving higher productivity and optimized outcome. Thus, workflow automation is simply a way of letting the software device and implement workflow system based on a set of key elements.

Workflow automation encompasses the following key elements:

- Triggers – Are the starter keys in the workflow process. For example, scrolling or pointing the mouse cursor towards the end of a web page or hovering the cursor towards exiting the page can trigger a landing page. This landing page could request you to subscribe to a newsletter, get downloadable freebies or grab an offer.

- Conditions – Are scenario-based rules that determine what action should be taken in case a certain scenario (event) happens. In its simplest form, a condition is structured in the form of "If 'X' is true, do 'A'. If 'X' is false, do 'B'. Otherwise, do 'C' "

- Actions – Actions refer to what should be done in case a given scenario occurs. For example, 'A' and 'B' above, are actions to be carried out based on the occurrence of 'X' and 'Y' events. Action 'C' above is an action to be taken in case neither events 'X' nor 'Y' happens.

- Delays – a delay is simply a time lag between two steps or actions within a workflow. This allows clear demarcation between them so that errors are avoided. It also allows maturity of an occurrence before an action is taken or the maturity of an action before another action is taken in response to a subsequent occurrence.

How workflows can be used in marketing automation

Workflows can be used to:

- Nurture Leads
- Incentivize feedback
- Up-sell customers

Benefits of workflow automation

Workflow automation is an enterprise-wide process. We can have a look at the general, marketing, and sales benefits.

General benefits of workflow automation:

- Higher visibility and analysis of the current business process
- Better communication
- Enhance collaboration
- Expanded mobility
- Faster response time
- Greater efficiency in operations
- More accountability
- Reduced errors
- Lower costs

Benefits of workflow automation to Marketing:

- Enhanced consistency in lead management
- Filtering, sieving, value-addition, and enrichment of content and other processes that require several stages of verification and approval

- Boosted collaboration between various marketing teams in multiple locations
- Setting up and triggering multiple autopilot campaigns and monitoring their performance through a unified dashboard
- Consigning menial and repetitive tasks to the automated system thus freeing up human creativity

Benefits of workflow automation to sales:

- No lead accidentally escapes due to inadvertent human error
- A unified response to qualified leads
- Customized content creation and delivery
- Shorter sales cycle
- Simplified list building through the standardized process
- Higher quality customer engagement
- Greater analysis, reporting, and insight into the on-going process

HOW MUCH CONTROL SHOULD I HAVE IN THE BUSINESS AFTER AUTOMATION?

Having control is a great function of leadership and management. Without control, managing people, systems and resources become virtually impossible. Thus, the concern of any leader and manager is how to ensure that whichever system is implemented, there is no loss of control. The alternative to control is chaos and anarchy, which no business enterprise would desire to fall into or entertain.

Marketing automation does not substitute you. On the contrary, it complements you. It simply enables you to perform more effectively and efficiently towards optimizing your outcome. Thus, you are not ceding control of the marketing process, but you are simply delegating. Instead of delegating repetitive tasks to humans under your control, you delegate to machines under your control. Delegation is neither ceding control nor losing control. Instead, it is about having better control.

How to have effective control after automation

Automation helps you to free yourself from being extremely active to being extremely creative. In this regard, you gain more control over your business but in a highly creative way

- Report-based control
- Vision-based creative control
- Leadership

Report-based control

Automation tools provide sophisticated, intuitive and incisive reports. These reports help you to interpret your firm's performance and take appropriate control measures.

Vision-based creative control

With more time and effort freed up, you are able to focus more on visualizing the future of your enterprise and devising creative solutions. You can then implement control measures to ensure that your firm heads towards your vision and implements creative control parameters within the automated system to ensure that your vision is achieved.

Leadership

Automation frees more of your time that you would have otherwise spend on management and thus enable you to spend more of it towards leadership. You are able to focus less on the technical side of things are they are taken care of by automation and focus more on leadership.

Leadership enables you to set the firm's direction towards the achievement of your vision. Setting the firm's direction is in itself a soft and smart way of controlling your business.

WHEN IS THE RIGHT TIME TO START AUTOMATING?

Doing the right thing in the right way is the cardinal principle of any organized system. Furthermore, application of software technology obeys the common adage "garbage in, garbage out". Thus, the first rule to automation is streamlining your manual system to achieve efficient operations. Automation then comes in to magnify this efficiency. Otherwise, if you do not create an efficient operating system, you are more likely to magnify inefficiency.

You need to carry out thorough systems analysis in order to assess your current operations and your already deployed technology systems. This will enable you to identify needs that require investment in automation. You will also be able to establish as to whether you deserve automation tools for particular marketing function or an entire integrated automation platform.

What you must keep in mind is that automation is a great thing to do. However, like any other enterprise resource, doing it prematurely or without a properly identified need may not result in the desired ROI, which may simply mean that costs will outweigh the benefits.

To be well guided, you need to establish critical indicators that will signal to you that it is now the right time to venture into marketing automation.

Indicators that your business needs marketing automation

The two most important indicators are:

1. Your enterprise size
2. Automation needs

Your enterprise Size

As a rule of thumb, marketing automation will be suitable for your firm if it has:

- A well-defined, elaborate and process-driven communication system
- A large database of subscribers, customers, or leads
- An annual gross turnover in excess of $100,000

Automation needs

The following are telling signs that your firm needs marketing automation:

- Your time and cost of sales and marketing keeps on increasing as your revenue grows
- Your firm is not optimizing on its up-selling or cross-selling potential
- There is a high level of inconsistency in handling your leads
- There is lower than potential level of customer retention
- Your sales team seems to be overwhelmed by its manual response to inquiries
- You are manually sending bulk newsletters, and this is grabbing up a lot of staff time and cost
- Your sales process needs to be streamlined.

Indicators that the sales process needs to be streamlined

- There is inconsistency in communication between the sales team and various market segments teams in terms of what conversation should take place based on the various lead and buyer behavior scenarios
- There is lack of efficient content strategy mapped to the buyer's journey
- The sales team is overwhelmed in handling the high number of leads being passed to them

- There is lack of an effective mechanism of tracking leads' digital body language across various channels and touch points
- The lead nurturing effort is stunted and needs to be scaled up to match the potential

Indicators that your firm is not optimizing its up-scaling and cross-scaling potential

1. The leads exceed marketing capacity to handle
2. Low conversion rate despite the high volume of leads

The low conversion rate can be remedied by:

- Improving the quality of leads
- Improving the follow-up process

Automated lead scoring tools can help separate quality leads from non-quality leads so that you do not waste your energy on non-quality leads. Instead, the effort that would have otherwise been wasted on non-quality leads is redirected to quality leads thus boosting their nurture.

Lead capturing tools can help increase the volume of quality leads through customized landing pages, customized content curation, and event-triggered response actions.

Follow-up process can be automated by use of CRM software. This will ensure that cold, warm, and hot leads are taken care of through customized and targeted lead nurturing based on their actions and behaviors.

Market automation as part of the market expansion strategy

There are those situations whereby your manual system is still serving you efficiently and effectively. However, you have a strategy to rapidly scale up your marketing operations such that you anticipate either that the current system cannot cope or it would be more expensive to cope and thus cheaper to automate. This calls for the early adoption of automation so that your marketing system become acclimatized to automated operations early enough prior to the expansion burst.

This adoption strategy will lead to:

- **Acquiring the right software** – Early adoption of marketing automation allows you an opportunity to do extensive research in order to acquire the right software. It also grants you an opportunity to have thorough testing of the various pieces of software before narrowing down to what works best for your unique needs. Through research and testing, you are able to find an automation system that fits well with your existing technologies and processes. This ensures seamless integration, as you are able to handle compatibility issues well in advance.

- **Quality database** – As you transition to an automated system, you will have to reorganize your database so that it is streamlined and free from dead ends.

- **Better content management** – Most content automation tools have much better content curation features than what you would achieve manually. Thus, with early adoption of content automation tools, you are able to improve gradually on your content curation, distribution, and management.

- **The increased volume of qualified leads** – Having the right automation software, quality database and better content management, you have a higher chance of capturing more leads. Yet, with lead scoring features that come with CRM software, you will be able to have a higher volume of quality leads than you would achieve with a manual system.

- **Increased efficiency** – Early adoption of automation brings about more effective and efficient utilization of marketing resources. You are able to rationalize your staff and retain those that can add creative value to your marketing process as most repetitive tasks are surrendered to machines. Machines are more adept at repetitive tasks than human beings are. Through automation, you are able to minimize errors that inadvertently arise due to manually repetitive tasks.

- **Better ROI** – With increasing volume of quality leads and greater nurturing effort through the CRM, you can achieve higher conversion rates, which lead to more revenue. On the cost side, you are able to eliminate unnecessary labor costs and thus have lower overall marketing cost. Marketers are freed up to creative endeavors such as understanding customers' needs and coming up creative solutions. This increases the net yield on your marketing investment and hence higher ROI.

Marketing automation as part of your market expansion strategy grants you the significant time required to understand all software features of your preferred automation solution. It also grants you time to experience a complete clarity of your marketing process during the test phase with free trial versions.

Where do you start if your business firm has never used any digital marketing system?

In case your company has never used any digital marketing system, then there is a lot to learn and acclimatize with before venturing into automation. Automation is ideal for those who have worked with various separate digital marketing tools.

The best way to begin is to start with the non-automated traditional forms of digital marketing to better prepare your marketing process. Use search engine optimization tools, keyword research tools, social media marketing tools and email marketing tools. Later on, you can begin by automating email marketing, followed by automatic content curation. Afterward, you can automate social media marketing.

The experience gained in automating individual marketing functions can equip you with relevant skills and knowledge of what you deserve in an integrated automated marketing platform.

Reference: https://ozcontent.com/blog/12-benefits-of-marketing-automation/

CASE STUDIES: IMPLEMENTING MARKETING AUTOMATION

It is commonly said that experience is the best teacher. Yet, wise are those who learn from other people's experiences. Case Studies are the best way to learn about other people's implementations before attempting to implement a given tool or system.

In this Section, we will explore various case studies related to the implementation of marketing automation.

Case 1: Paper Style (paperstyle.com)

Paper Style is a stationery specialist that provides items for special occasions such as wedding occasions.

Pain point

The challenge was how to provide a customized and personalized response based on customer behavior.

Automation solution: Personalized content

The marketing automation campaign targeted brides-to-be, brides, friends of brides, with personalized content/response based on their interactive behavior on the website and with emails sent to them.

Implementation

PaperStyle focused on three touch points:

- A visit to a wedding-related page on paperstyle.com – this triggered customized landing page
- Wedding links in emails – A click triggered personalized action
- Purchases – A purchase of a bridal shower or wedding product triggered a personalized action e.g. cross-selling (recommendation of complementary items)

Results:

Paper Style decided to move from generic newsletter to personalized marketing automation. This resulted in:

- 244% increase in click rates
- 161% increase in email click rates
- 330% increase in revenue per mailing

Case 2: Acteva

Acteva is a specialist in online registration, payment management, and ticketing service.

The pain point

Lack of sufficient visibility

Automation solution: Lead nurturing

Acteva wanted a marketing automated solution that would greatly increase its visibility. It was already using Salesforce to improve its targeting and ROI.

Implementation

The company engaged Marketo to offer integration with its Salesforce tool to enhance:

- Lead nurturing
- Customized landing pages
- Email campaigns

Results:

- 60% cut in time
- 70% cut in cost
- 350% increase in marketing ROI
- 100% growth in automated sectors

- $2 million increase in gross revenue

Case 3: Opsview

Opsview is a software company that provides enterprise-level monitoring and management of IT infrastructure

Pain point

The challenge was distinguishing between two types of leads:

- Those that were contented
- Those who desired extra service such as software downloads and/or white papers

Automation solution: Lead nurturing/scoring

Opsview wanted to have a lead score system that would enable to determine which leads to push over to the sales team for further nurturing.

Implementation

The company decided to have a lead score of 26 as the break off point such that only leads with a score of 26 and above would be sent to the sales team for further action.

Results:

- The volume of quality leads to the sales department increased by 55%
- Pre-qualification leads went up by 30%
- Revenue grew by 178%

Case 4: Cincom Systems

Cincom Systems is an enterprise software solutions provider.

Pain point

Trouble in identifying newsletter subscribers in the sales process and converting leads to sales.

Automation solution: Lead management

Lead generation, lead scoring and lead nurturing through targeted campaigns.

Implementation

Implementation was carried out in five phases:

Phase 1: Tracking users based on information captured during their clicks.

Phase 2: Tag each article based on the subject matter and use the tags as indicators of whether a subscriber is interested or not, in what is being provided.

Phase 3: Carry out a content audit in order to evaluate and analyze the company's podcasts, blogs, eBooks, and websites in order to identify content that worked best for their readers and understand the reasons for it.

Phase 4: Unleashing marketing campaign to have a clearer perspective of readers through progressive profiling. For example, each time a prospect engaged with the company's offers, the prospect would be asked more and deeper questions. Each answer provided would help to generate a clearer picture of the prospect.

Phase 5: Make follow-up campaign to pursue potential leads based on the lead score generated out of the information gathered.

Results:

- 1941% increase in the click-to-open rate
- 256% improvement in the campaign open rate
- An average of 18 new sales leads per week

- 1513 new potential opportunities identified

Case 5: Dormify

Dormify deals with creative and artistic lifestyle products where university students can buy them online for their university dorm.

Pain point

- Low email marketing lead conversion
- A large young audience with highly diverse personalities, tastes, preferences, and styles
- Lack of marketing system to provide a customized solution for each of these personalities, tastes, preferences, and styles

Automation solution: CRM automation

Dormify required a CRM automation system that would allow segmentation of the young audience. This segmentation would be based on their personalities, tastes, preferences, and styles but also cater to their parents who happen to fall into a different age bracket.

Implementation

The following were implemented:

- Streamlined email process

- Market segmentation
- Personalized email journey
- Customized response based on reaction to the email
- Follow-up on cart abandonment midway
- Post-purchase follow-up

Results:

- 42% increase in the duration of site visits
- 20% more site page views
- 19% increase in email revenue
- Two times conversion rate of email visitors

Case 6: MacAfee

MacAfee is an internationally reputed online security and antivirus company.

Pain point

High volume of leads yet extremely poor conversion rate due to a high percentage of poor quality leads.

Automation solution: Lead management and streamlined operations

Marketing automation was needed to help the marketing department get higher quality leads with higher conversion potential. Furthermore, a disconnection between marketing (lead generation and lead nurturing) and sales department (lead conversion) existed due to disjointed goals.

Implementation

Marketing automation process helped to streamline operations between marketing and sales and thus brought them to align their goals.

- Market segmentation helped to create personalized campaigns
- Lead scoring helped to sieve off low-quality leads by the marketing department thus enabling only quality leads to be nurtured with follow-up campaigns.
- Only hot leads were transferred to the sales department for conversion

Results:

- 35% overall drop in lead volume
- More quality leads
- Four times increase in lead conversion rate

- Increase in up-sell and cross-sales
- Improvement in alignment between marketing and sales departments

Case 7: Thomas Reuters

Thomas Reuters is an international news outlet.

Pain point

A disconnect between marketing and sales department thus leading to loss of lots of potential leads along the sales funnel. They could not even identify these leads, as they had not defined them.

Automation solution: Lead management

It was clearly apparent that lead management system was lacking and had to be built up and automated in order to heal the pain points.

Implementation

In the implementation process, it became imperative that both the marketing and sales departments had to come together and collaborate in defining what a lead was – a prerequisite for lead generation process. They also had to create a distinction between quality leads and poor leads – a prerequisite for lead scoring. This way, lead scoring could become possible – a prerequisite for lead nurturing and lead conversion.

After defining the leads and identifying lead scoring criteria, an automated lead management system was implemented which not only helped in streamlining the sales process but also created intelligent analytics that enabled both marketing and sales creatively contribute towards the same goal – higher conversion rate and greater revenues.

Alignment of sales and marketing, improved segmentation and targeting brought highly positive results.

Results:

- 23% increase in quality leads
- 72% drop in lead conversion time
- 175% increase in revenues attributed to marketing leads

Case 8: Salesforce

Salesforce is a global marketing technology provider.

Pain point

Low visibility in the UK market

Automation solution: Content marketing automation

To boost visibility in the UK market, Salesforce engaged a strategy that encompassed content marketing, social marketing, and search marketing.

Implementation

Six user profiles were created and each assigned to different stages of the buying cycle to optimize content strategy.

Results:

- 2,500% increase in social traffic
- 80% increase in overall traffic
- Over 10,000 eBook downloads and sales leads

Case 9: Capterra

Capterra is an online company that focuses on providing information on various technology solutions.

Pain point

Low volume of qualifying leads.

Automation solution: Lead management

A lead management system that would cut down on time spent by sales team on lead management

Implementation:

A special API was created that fed all their leads into their market automation system. Drip emails were produced to reactivate unresponsive leads, boost email contact, and discard post qualification checks.

Results:

- 400% improvements in qualification rate at the same close rate
- 94% reduction in average response time

Case 10: SmartBear Software

SmartBear Software is a mobile software company providing B2B cloud mobile solutions.

Pain point

Low marketing capabilities to cope up with rapidly growing leads.

Implementation

Marketing automation system was considered with the following key objectives:

- Scalability
- CRM integration
- Ease of use

With automation in place, email campaigns were released and lead management was put in place to handle an increasingly high volume of leads in different product categories.

Results:

- 200% increase in lead volume
- 80% generation of global leads through automated trial downloads
- 85% revenue was generated by the trial downloads

WHICH AUTOMATION TOOLS ARE BEST FOR YOU?

It is great to carry out marketing automation. However, it is far more important to have the right tools. Choosing the right tools depends on several factors.

Factors that will help you determine the right automation tools

The following are the important factors that will help you determine the kind of tools that you need:

1. The size of your enterprise
2. The core marketing functions that you seek to prioritize in your automation endeavor
3. The automation budget at your disposal
4. Ability to integrate with your already existing software infrastructure

Features to look for in your automation tools

Not all automation tools are created equal. Thus, very few will have all the features. This too will be reflected in the required budget match the large size of features. Hence, there are times you will require trade-offs by looking for automation tools that meet your top priorities but within your budget.

The following are features to look out for based on your priority criteria:

- **Email marketing automation** – This is usually the highest priority area for marketing automation since the biggest potential of online leads comes from email marketing. What you should look for is whether the tool supports drip email campaign, demographic segmentation, and subject line A/B testing.

- **CRM automation**– Customer relationship management is critical to converting potential leads into customers and building customer loyalty. You should give priority to a tool that has inbuilt CRM system. Alternatively, find a one that has the capability of seamlessly integrating with your preferred standalone CRM tool. This CRM system should be able to allow advanced tagging and lead scoring.

- **Content marketing automation** – Content is king. Content is what provides potential leads with information that inspires them and directs their buyer behavior into preferred positive action. A good tool should have the ability to enable you to create customized landing pages based on potential leads' behavioral segmentation, create or distribute webinars, curate content, and distribute content to multiple channels.

- **Social media automation** – Social media has become extremely important in terms of brand visibility, awareness, and recognition. It has also become a good source of potential leads. This means that social media cannot be ignored in any online marketing effort. A social media automation tool should enable you to handle multiple social media channels (e.g. Facebook, Twitter, Google Plus, etc) at a centralized dashboard. From this centralized dashboard, you can be able to create uniquely customized posts for various channels and segments, schedule and post them. You should also be able to engage the audience through multiple channels from the same dashboard. More importantly, you should be able to gather marketing intelligence through the various social media analytics report gathered. Lastly, but not least, you should be able to create targeted advertising to various social media channels from the same dashboard. Depending on your budget, you may need to trade-off some features for what works most at your given budget.

- **E-commerce marketing automation** –This feature is great for you if you are a trader (probably has an online store). However, this customization will not be readily available on all marketing automation platforms since not all businesses are trade-oriented. Nonetheless, if you have an online store, this is a great deal. You can easily integrate and streamline your sales and marketing automation right from branding, lead generation, eventual sale and after-sale support.

- **Training and support** – Most marketing automation platforms require some level of user training in order to effectively utilize their facilities. This becomes more important if the platform is a self-hosted one since installation and setup will have to be done by the business firm rather than the platform vendor. There should be an elaborate multimedia user manual supported by user cases, white papers, topical articles, feature articles, and FAQs (Frequently Asked Questions). There should also be a facility for technical support such as support tickets, support chats, live calls, among others.

Types of automation tools

There are many ways to classify automation tools. However, the following are the main categories of automation tools:

- Free
- Paid

- Open source
- Self-hosted
- Function-based
- Integrated platforms

Free automation tools

These tools are either free or have some free packages which you can upgrade to a paid package for better features. The following are some free automation tools:

1. MailChimp

Email marketing automation tool. Has a free basic package. There is a paid package for more advanced features.

Features bundled with the free option:

- In-built sign-up forms
- Automatic ad triggers and email triggers
- Newsletter templates
- Up to 2,000 subscribers
- No contract, no payment information required, or expiring trial
- Up to 12,000 emails per month
- Performance analytics and reporting

2. Hubspot

Features bundled with the free option:

- In-built forms
- Contact management
- Contact activity log for up to 7 days
- Lead workflows
- Lead analytics dashboard
- Insights into the company and its contacts

3. Vbout

Features bundled with the free option:

- Unlimited contacts
- Up to 1,000 emails per month
- Up to 2 customer journeys
- Up to 2 social media management profiles
- Up to 2 landing page options
- Insightful marketing analytics and reporting

4. Drip

Features bundled with the free option:

- Unlimited users
- Opt-in widgets for emails
- API access
- Third-Party Integrations
- Lead scoring capabilities
- Up to 100 subscribers

- Unlimited email sends
- Automated email marketing

5. Leadsius

Features bundled with the free option:

- 250 contacts
- 1 user
- Form and landing page creator (unlimited)
- Email creator and templates
- List management (static only, no dynamic lists)
- Reporting – emails, forms, web analytics
- Support – knowledge base and community support

6. Jumplead

Features bundled with the free option:

- Live chat support
- 1 user
- 200 contacts
- 100 emails
- 200 website visitors

7. SalesAutoPilot

Features bundled with the free option:

- Email automation
- 400 emails per month

- Sales automation (A/B testing, landing pages, event-triggered action, etc)
- CRM module
- E-commerce module
- Helpdesk module
- Telemarketing support
- Personalized pdf
- Text message sending
- Affiliate module
- 1 user

8. Mautic

Features bundled with the free option:

- Leads management (monitoring and nurturing)
- Landing pages
- List building
- Email creation
- Analytics reports

9. Pimcore

Features bundled with the free option:

- Social media integration

- Email marketing
- Targeting
- A/B testing
- Analytics and reporting

10.   OpenEMM

Features bundled with the free option:

- Contact database
- Email template creation
- List management
- Event-triggered actions
- Targeting
- Analytics and reporting

Paid automation tools

Almost all the mentioned tools in this section (including the free ones) have a paid plan.

Open source automation tools

'Open source' simply means that the codes used in making the tools are open for viewing. This is a great benefit for those with the programming knowledge to tweak the tools to suit their own unique needs.

The following are the common open source marketing automation tools:

- Mautic
- Pimcore
- OpenEMM
- CampaignChain

Self-hosted automation tools

- Mautic
- SugarCRM Community Edition
- WP-CRM

Function-based automation tools

- Email marketing
- CRM
- Lead management
- E-commerce
- Social media marketing
- Content marketing

Email marketing automation:

- ActOn
- Zoho
- Custiomer.io

Lead Management automation:

- Sugar CRM
- Zoho CRM
- Salesforce Sales Cloud
- Hubspot CRM
- Pipedrive CRM
- ProsperWorks CRM

E-commerce automation:

- Klaviyo
- Windsor Cycle
- Hubspot
- Leadsquared
- GreenRope
- Kevy

Social media marketing automation:

- Hootsuite
- Sproutsocial

- Angora Pulse
- Social Pilot
- Mention
- Buffer

Content marketing automation:

- Eloqua
- Hubspot
- Act-On
- Inboundio

Integrated Marketing Automation platforms

Automation platforms comprise several integrated tools that offer a range of marketing automation solutions. They have all or almost all of the common features mentioned above for marketing automation tools.

The following are the most common marketing automation platform

- Hubspot
- Marketo
- ONTRAPORT

- Pardot
- Eloqua
- Act-On
- Mautic
- Autopilot
- Infusion
- Active Campaign

We can have a glimpse of the five most widely used marketing automation platforms – Hubspot, Marketo, ONTRAPORT, Autopilot, Infusionsoft, and Active Campaign.

HubSpot

Hubspot is an integrated automated marketing platform that is famed for its CRM billed "an automated solution to what salespeople hate – repetitive tasks".

The CRM automatically tracks and captures customer's entire journey through relevant data compilation. All this is made visible on a single centralized dashboard. The CRM intelligently tracks a specific customer's touch-points across multiple channels and keeps a log of emails, meetings, and calls.

Apart from its highly reputed CRM, it has other facilities such as landing pages, lead management, blogging, social media, web, SEO, ads email, and integration with Salesforce. This enables it to create personalized purchasing paths and uses compiled data to highlight the contribution of every marketing campaign to the sales basket.

The dashboard enables different marketing teams to immediately sort contracts – either won or not and have a clear view of their performance towards their set goals.

Marketo

Marketo is a relatively newer yet popular marketing automation platform reputed for its account-based marketing, digital ads, web, social, mobile, and email analytics. This provides an opportunity for business firms to drive engagements across multiple channels from a single platform.

Marketo has highly customized solutions for media, financial services, higher education, healthcare, technology, and manufacturing. The Engagement Hub intelligently collects data from various channels and touch-points from which it compiles, synthesizes and analyzes to provide coherent reports and rich various customer profiles. This enables business enterprises to adapt to the various market situations and personalize their interactions.

The highly sophisticated cloud-based infrastructure allows Marketo to handle millions of activities per day. It has a high capability that enables it to scale up with the customers' growth rates in terms of volume and needs. It aims at enabling small enterprises to develop and sustain long-lasting relationships with their customers through intelligent engagements.

ONTRAPORT

ONTRAPORT is primarily focused on intelligent data gathering, advanced analytics, and in-depth reporting with the aim enabling small business firms have a comprehensive visualization of their customer journey.

ONTRAPORT distinguishes itself as walking with small-scale businesses from the darkness of informational blindness to the light of intelligent visualization with the aim of enabling them to comprehend how each marketing effort is paying off. Its system helps customers see how customers respond to messages via multiple channels – postcards, landing pages, email, and SMS, among others – through data visualization.

Campaign Builder allows business firms to set specific goals and anchor their automation towards the achievement of those goals through high-level customizations. This combined with powerful insights enables customers to see the outcomes of their past efforts and be able to forecast how their future will turn out based on the various scenario simulations.

Infusionsoft

Infusionsoft offers automated marketing technology solutions that target small-scale businesses with the aim of fueling their growth. This technology offers CRM, e-commerce, mobile integration and various other integrations. It seeks to integrate its system with user's other systems to offer a wholesome synergy.

Infusionsoft solutions include lead capture, follow-up based user activity behavior and personalization based on customer behavior analytics. Like ONTRAPORT, it aims to lead small-scale businesses to the light of creative data visualization so that they can be able to track their historical marketing effort, identify what works and what does not work, seek the ROI on their current campaigns and be able to forecast future performance based on the trends.

ActiveCampaign

ActiveCampaign is largely focused on email automation while extending its set of technologies to other areas of marketing such as CRM, and SMS. Its primary goal is to enable marketers to boost yield from their email communication and engagements.

It has technologies that enable it to listen and learns email interactions with a view of rendering customized messages to prospects with the aim of converting them into customers and eventually product's advocates.

ActiveCampaign has a multichannel view that enables small businesses to have a glimpse of the marketing activities on their website, email, and mobile devices. It enables businesses to tap into its Campaign Builder to design highly impactful segment-targeted marketing campaigns based on intelligent analytics capture through multiple channels.

Autopilot

Autopilot boasts of being one of the simplest and easy-to-use customer-friendly marketing automation platforms. Autopilot aims at enabling marketers to trigger new relationships and rekindle old ones. It achieves this through sophisticated lead generation mechanism based on data captured and intelligence from customer's websites, self-service platforms offering postcards, in-app messages, email, and SMS.

Autopilot easily integrates with other automation tools to provide market segmentation and personalization of messages customized to target a particular market segment. It has great data analytics and reporting that allows marketers to have a deeper insight of the customers' journeys and monitor the performance of each journey with the aim of creating higher conversions.

CONCLUSION

Thank you for acquiring and reading this book.

Lack of adequate information has been the biggest obstacle, especially for small businesses when it comes to the need for marketing automation. This book has deliberately endeavored to fill this informational gap.

I hope the information provided to you in this book has enabled you to embrace marketing automation for your business. It is also my sincere hope that you have been inspired enough to share with others information about this book so that they too can acquire a copy of it for their own reference.

Good luck!

www.ingramcontent.com/pod-product-compliance
Lightning Source LLC
Chambersburg PA
CBHW061050220326
41597CB00018BA/2729